MINDFULNESS RECLAIMED

FROM CHAOS TO CLARITY IN 21 INTENTIONAL DAYS

STHITIPRAGYAN MOHANTY

To every soul who has ever felt lost in the noise—
may you find your stillness again.

To the wounded hearts and restless minds—
this is a gentle reminder: you are not broken, just waiting to be heard.

To my teachers, seen and unseen—
thank you for awakening the light within me.

To my tribe of changemakers, seekers, and believers—
your courage to feel, heal, and transform inspires every word in these pages.

And to the child within each of us—
may you forever remember how to return home to yourself.

Contents

Foreword

In a world that rarely pauses, stillness has become a forgotten language.

We live in times where the external demands our attention endlessly—yet the real answers lie within. Mindfulness Reclaimed is not just a book; it's an invitation. An invitation to return. To reconnect To remember.

Through the pages ahead, you will not find prescriptions or perfection. Instead, you'll uncover practices, reflections, and insights born from lived experience—one breath, one moment at a time. This book doesn't promise to change your life overnight. It offers something deeper: the tools to reclaim your inner space, to navigate chaos with clarity, and to come home to yourself.

The wisdom within these pages is rooted in ancient practices, modern understanding, and a deep reverence for the human spirit's resilience. It's a guide for anyone who is ready to meet themselves—honestly, gently, and with open arms.

May this book be your companion in silence, your reminder in struggle, and your mirror in moments of awakening.

With grace and gratitude,
Sthitipragyan Mohanty

Preface

I didn't set out to write a book on mindfulness. In truth, I once resisted the very idea. Like many people, I associated mindfulness with something trendy — a buzzword floating through wellness circles, often detached from its roots and reduced to quick-fix breathing techniques.

But life, as it tends to do, had other plans.

In the midst of personal chaos — grief, burnout, and an overwhelming sense of disconnection — I found myself sitting alone in silence. No apps. No mantras. Just breath and discomfort. And it was there, in the raw simplicity of the present moment, that mindfulness reclaimed me.

I began reading ancient texts alongside neuroscience journals. I practiced mindfulness not as a task, but as a way of being. Slowly, I began to rebuild my life around presence. That experience became the seed for this book.

This is not a textbook, nor is it a step-by-step manual. It's a living exploration — part memoir, part guide, part invitation. You'll find spiritual reflections drawn from traditions like Buddhism and Stoicism, paired with modern psychology and grounded, practical tools.

The path back to mindfulness is not linear. It's layered, cyclical, and deeply personal. But I believe that in reclaiming the present moment, we reclaim something far more essential — our wholeness.

May this book serve you as a gentle companion on your own journey home.

Warm Regards

Sthitipragyan Mohanty

Stillness in Meditation

"यथादीपोनविातस्थोनङ्गतसोपमास्मृता।
योगनियतचत्तितस्ययुञ्जतोयोगमात्मनः॥"
— *BHAGAVAD GITA 6.19*
*Just as a lamp in a windless place does not flicker, so is
the mind of the yogi who is united with the Self in
meditation.*

Mindfulness Living

Table of Contents

 This structure offers depth, flexibility, and emotional continuity — a journey that begins with awareness and ends with embodiment

INTRODUCTION TO MINDFULNESS

The Art of Returning

In the soft hush of dawn, before the mind has fully woken and the world begins to call for our attention, there is a moment. A single breath, unburdened by thought. A heartbeat, undistracted by urgency. This moment — simple, quiet, unassuming — is where mindfulness lives.

Mindfulness, at its core, is not a technique. It is a way of being. A returning — again and again — to what is already here.

What Is Mindfulness, Really?

The word mindfulness is everywhere these days. It's in apps, workplace policies, Instagram captions, and wellness retreats. But despite its growing popularity, its meaning often gets diluted.

Mindfulness originates from the Pali word sati, which means to remember, to be aware, to be present. In Buddhist philosophy, mindfulness is not separate from wisdom or compassion — it is the very foundation upon which these qualities arise.

Scientifically, mindfulness is defined as the ability to maintain moment-to-moment awareness of our thoughts, feelings, bodily sensations, and surrounding environment — without judgment. Neuroscientific research shows that consistent mindfulness practice can reshape the brain, reduce stress, and enhance emotional regulation.

But even with all the data and definitions, mindfulness is best understood through direct experience — through stillness, through noticing, through simply being.

The Modern Dilemma: A Mind Divided

In a world built on speed and productivity, our attention is constantly fragmented. We scroll while we eat. We text while we walk. We listen while planning our next reply. Our minds are seldom here.

This division comes at a cost. Anxiety, burnout, loneliness, and chronic distraction have become the norm. We've gained technology but lost connection — to nature, to each other, to ourselves.

Mindfulness is not a luxury in these times; it is a necessary act of rebellion. A sacred pause in a culture that glorifies doing over being.

The Promise of Presence

What happens when we begin to live with presence?

We start to notice the warmth of sunlight on skin. The flavor of a single bite. The rise and fall of breath. We respond to life rather than react to it. We reclaim the richness of each moment, not by adding anything new, but by peeling away the layers of noise that separate us from the now.

From ancient monks to modern scientists, the consensus is clear: presence heals, connects, and transforms.

A Practice, Not Perfection

Mindfulness is not about being calm all the time. It's not about banishing thoughts or emotions. It's about turning toward each moment with openness and curiosity — even the messy ones.

Some days, presence will feel effortless. Other days, it will be a struggle. That's okay. Every breath is a chance to begin again.

CHAPTER TWO

RECLAIMING THE PRESENT MOMENT

Healing Begins Where Awareness Meets Compassion

There is a moment — subtle yet profound — when we realize that we've been living elsewhere. Our body may be here, but our mind is scattered across past regrets, future worries, and unresolved stories. Mindfulness invites us back into presence — not to escape those stories, but to reclaim them, and in doing so, to reclaim ourselves.

But what exactly are we reclaiming?

We are reclaiming the self that was left behind. The inner child whose voice was never heard. The emotions we numbed to survive. The joy we postponed until it was "safe." And most of all, we are reclaiming the power of now — the only moment where true healing can happen.

The Body Remembers. The Mind Reacts. The Heart Waits.

Stress isn't just in the mind; it's etched into the nervous system. Chronic stress conditions us to stay in survival mode — fight, flight, freeze — and in that state, we lose touch with our wholeness. Our breath becomes shallow, our thoughts race, and presence slips through our fingers.

Mindfulness acts as a bridge — connecting body, mind, and heart. It helps us notice when we've left ourselves. When we begin to pause, to breathe deeply, we allow the body to soften and the nervous system to reset. From that stillness, deeper layers begin to surface — including the voice of our inner child.

Who Is the Inner Child?

Your inner child is not just a metaphor. It is the collection of your earliest memories, emotions, and unmet needs. It's the part of you that learned to shrink, to hide, to perform, or to rebel — just to feel safe or loved.

When we ignore this part of ourselves, it speaks through emotional reactivity, self-sabotage, or chronic anxiety. But when we turn toward the inner child with mindfulness and compassion, healing begins.

Mindfulness allows us to hear the quiet whispers:

"I'm scared."

"I'm tired of pretending."

"I just want to be held."

And from that space of awareness, we can finally respond — not with judgment, but with gentleness.

Mindfulness as an Act of Inner Parenting

Imagine being the wise, grounded adult your younger self never had. That's what mindfulness makes possible.

Every time you pause instead of reacting, breathe instead of lashing out, or listen to your feelings instead of numbing them — you're reparenting your inner child. You're saying:

"I see you now. I'm here. You are safe."

This is how stress transforms into self-awareness. How pain becomes purpose. How presence becomes power.

A Practice: The Inner Child Check-In

Set a timer for 5–10 minutes. Sit somewhere quiet. Place a hand over your heart or belly.

Gently ask yourself:

- What does my inner child need from me right now?
- When did I last feel triggered or stressed?
- Was that moment connected to an older wound?

Just notice. No fixing, no forcing. Just be with what arises. Breathe.

Stress Is a Signal, Not a Sentence

Mindfulness doesn't erase stress — it rewrites your relationship to it. Instead of being swept away, you learn to watch it rise and fall. You learn to ask:

- Is this stress protecting something?
- What's beneath this tension?
- Can I meet this moment with curiosity instead of fear?

Reclaiming the present means honoring every part of it — even the uncomfortable. Because healing doesn't happen in the future. It happens now.

The next chapter will explore the spiritual and practical foundations of mindful living — the inner architecture that supports this transformation.

CHAPTER THREE

THE PILLARS OF MINDFUL LIVING

Building Inner Sanctuary in a Restless World

To live mindfully is to build a life on sacred ground — moment by moment, breath by breath. It is not about perfection, but about presence. Not about changing who we are, but about remembering who we've always been beneath the noise.

There are certain spiritual and psychological pillars that form the architecture of a mindful life. When practiced consistently, these principles bring us back to our center — especially when life feels chaotic, overwhelming, or painful.

Let's explore five core pillars that support a mindful, soul-aligned way of living.

1. Awareness: The Doorway to the Now

Awareness is the foundation. Without it, we are asleep — driven by habit, unconscious patterns, and old wounds. With it, we wake up. We begin to notice:

- The tightening in our chest when we feel unseen
- The moment we start people-pleasing to avoid conflict
- The stories we inherited that no longer serve us

Awareness is not just intellectual — it is embodied. It lives in the breath, in the gut, in the whisper of intuition. And the more we practice, the more clearly we hear it.

Mindful Practice: Try labeling your inner experience in real time: "I'm noticing tension," or "I feel overwhelmed." Naming what's present helps to bring it into the light.

2. Acceptance: The Ground of Healing

Awareness without acceptance can feel harsh. This is where many people stop — they see their patterns and judge themselves for them.

True mindfulness involves radical self-acceptance. It doesn't mean resignation; it means meeting what is real without trying to escape it.

Especially in inner child healing, acceptance sounds like:

- "Yes, that hurt me."
- "Yes, I carried shame that wasn't mine."
- "Yes, I still feel fear sometimes — and that's okay."

We stop fighting reality and start holding it with care.

Mindful Practice: When a painful emotion arises, place your hand on your chest and say softly, "This, too, belongs." Let the resistance soften.

3. Intention: The Heart Behind Presence

Intention brings direction to our awareness. It's the "why" behind our practice. Without intention, we drift. With it, we root.

Ask yourself:

- Why do I want to be more mindful?
- Who am I becoming through this path?
- What does my inner child need to feel safe and loved?

Let your intention guide your actions, your rituals, your daily choices.

Mindful Practice: Write down one word each morning that defines your intention (e.g., "peace," "honesty," "nurture"). Return to it throughout the day.

4. Compassion: The Medicine of the Soul

You cannot punish yourself into wholeness. Healing requires compassion — especially for the younger you, the overwhelmed you, the parts of you still in hiding.

Compassion is the antidote to shame. It is the balm that says:

- "You did the best you could."
- "I see your pain — and I won't abandon you."
- "You are already enough."

Through compassion, mindfulness becomes a sanctuary, not a performance.

Mindful Practice: Try this inner child dialogue: "Little me, what do you need from me today?" Then sit quietly and wait for the answer.

5. Simplicity: The Space for Presence

We cannot be present when our lives are overcrowded. Simplicity isn't just about decluttering your closet — it's about creating emotional and mental space.

Simplicity may look like:

- Saying no to what drains you
- Logging off social media for a day
- Choosing fewer tasks with deeper focus
- Letting go of relationships that pull you out of alignment

Mindfulness thrives in simplicity. It's in the space between distractions where we finally hear ourselves.

Mindful Practice: Choose one area of life to simplify this week — your schedule, your environment, your inner dialogue.

CHAPTER FOUR

PRACTICAL TECHNIQUES & DAILY RITUALS

Transforming Presence into Practice

Integrating mindfulness into everyday life is less about dramatic changes and more about the gentle accumulation of small, intentional acts. In this chapter, we will explore a variety of practices — from grounding breathwork to reflective journaling — each designed to help you forge a closer connection with your inner self while managing stress and nurturing your inner child.

1. Breathwork for Centering and Calming

Our breath is the most accessible tool for returning to the present. When stress strikes, it's as if our breath stumbles into shallow spaces. Here are some techniques:

- Deep Diaphragmatic Breathing: Inhale slowly through your nose, letting your belly expand, and then exhale fully through your mouth. Imagine releasing tension with each exhalation.
- Box Breathing (Square Breathing): Inhale for a count of four, hold for four, exhale for four, and hold again for four. Visualize drawing a square in your mind, anchoring you in the rhythm of life.

A soothing illustration of gentle breath flow overlaid on a calm nature backdrop can reinforce these steps, guiding the reader as they practice.

2. Body Scans: Embracing Full Awareness

The body harbors emotions and memories, especially those of our inner child. A body scan allows you to gently explore and release tension:

- Guided Body Scan: Lie down in a comfortable space. Starting at your toes, slowly move your awareness upward. Notice any sensations without judgment — simply observe. If you detect discomfort, imagine breathing warmth and light into that area.

- Mindful Movement: Simple stretches or yoga poses can awaken your body's energy centers. With each movement, try to connect with sensations and emotions, nurturing the parts of you that may have felt forgotten.

A gentle illustration of someone lying or sitting in a peaceful pose amid soft natural light can serve as a visual guide to this practice.

3. Journaling: A Dialogue with the Self

When words flow onto paper, we create a conversation with the deeper parts of ourselves. Journaling can be both therapeutic and transformative:

- Free Writing: Set a timer for 10 minutes, and write without editing or judgment. Let your thoughts spill freely; this helps unearth underlying stressors or memories that need healing.
- Prompted Reflections: Use questions like, "What does my inner child need right now?" or "Where am I holding tension today?" Allow these prompts to guide your narrative.
- Gratitude Journaling: Note down three things you are grateful for each day. This practice can reframe your mindset and highlight everyday moments of beauty.

Integrate a visual element such as an open journal with handwritten notes and gentle watercolor accents that suggest creativity and openness.

4. Mindful Eating & Listening: Engaging All Senses

Mindfulness is not limited to meditation. It extends into every aspect of life, including how we nourish and communicate:

- Mindful Eating: Before each meal, take a moment to observe your food — its color, texture, and aroma. Eat slowly, savoring each bite as a part of a nourishing ritual.
- Mindful Listening: In conversations, practice active listening. Try to fully absorb what the other person is saying instead of formulating your response. This deepens connection and reduces miscommunication.

Visual cues for this section might include soft imagery of a mindful dining setting or a serene dialogue scene.

5. Creating a Daily Ritual

Establishing a personal ritual can anchor your day in mindfulness:

- Morning and Evening Practices: Begin your day with a few minutes of meditation or deep breathing, and wind down with reflective journaling or a body scan. Consistency builds a sacred routine.
- Dedicated Mindful Moments: Identify 'pause points' during your day — a break between tasks or a walk outside — to check in with yourself. Consider using a simple journal prompt or a mindfulness app during these moments.
- Mindfulness Reminders: Set gentle alarms or place physical reminders (like a small stone or a picture) in your environment to prompt you back into presence throughout the day.

Visual elements could include a series of icons or a gentle timeline diagram showing these ritual touch-points in a day.

6. Integrating Inner Child Healing

Throughout your daily practices, always return to the gentle voice of your inner child. Here are some specialized suggestions:

- Inner Child Meditation: Visualize meeting your younger self in a safe, quiet place. Speak kindly and reassure them, acknowledging both past pain and present healing.
- Self-Soothing Techniques: When anxiety or stress arises, find comfort by holding a soft object or wrapping yourself in a favorite blanket. Allow these physical sensations to remind you that safety and self-love are within reach.
- Daily Affirmations: Create affirmations that speak directly to inner child healing, such as "I am safe, I am loved, I am whole." Repeat them throughout your day to reinforce a mindset of nurturing care.

Consider placing small visual call-outs with inspirational affirmations or soft doodles that evoke the warmth of self-compassion

CHAPTER FIVE

MINDFULNESS & INNER CHILD HEALING

Meeting the Self That Still Waits to Be Seen

There is a younger version of you still living within — a quiet voice, a hidden ache, a deep longing. Often, we mistake anxiety, emotional reactivity, or self-doubt as flaws, when in truth, they're echoes of a child still waiting to be heard, seen, and embraced. Mindfulness becomes the light that guides us back to this forgotten self.

This chapter is a homecoming.

The Inner Child Lives in the Present

Your inner child does not live in your past. It lives in your present reactions — the moments of fear, defensiveness, or overgiving. These reactions are often survival patterns shaped during early experiences of feeling unsafe, unloved, or emotionally neglected.

Mindfulness brings compassionate awareness to these patterns. Instead of judging our responses, we begin to ask:

- Who in me is feeling this?
- What did I need back then that I can offer now?
- Can I hold this emotion without abandoning myself?

This is inner child healing. This is mindfulness reclaimed.

Signs Your Inner Child Is Calling Out

- You feel chronically unsafe, even when nothing is "wrong"
- You fear rejection or feel unworthy of love
- You over-apologize or struggle to say no
- You shut down in conflict or overreact emotionally
- You feel a persistent emptiness despite external success

These are not personal failings. These are invitations. Each is a doorway back to the parts of you that need nurturing.

The Role of Mindfulness in Inner Child Work

Traditional inner child work often uses therapy, visualization, or journaling. When paired with mindfulness, the work becomes even more profound.

Mindfulness allows us to:

- Pause when we're triggered instead of reacting
- Create space for emotions without suppression
- Recognize old patterns and consciously choose new ones
- Listen inwardly and respond with love, not shame

Mindful Inner Child Practices

1. Visualization: Safe Space Encounter

   - Imagine a quiet, beautiful place where your inner child feels safe.
   - Picture yourself entering and gently sitting beside your younger self.
   - Ask: "How are you feeling today?" Then just listen.
   - Offer loving, supportive words — the kind you wish you had heard growing up.

1. Compassionate Journaling

   - Write a letter from your adult self to your inner child.
   - Then, write back from your inner child's perspective.
   - Reflect on unmet needs and how you can now meet them lovingly.

3. Somatic Awareness

   - Notice where emotions land in your body.
   - Gently place your hand there and breathe into the sensation.
   - Say silently: "I'm here now. I'm listening."

4. Daily Affirmations for the Inner Child

   - "You are safe now."

- ◦ "You are loved and seen."
- ◦ "You don't have to earn your worth."

Integrating Healing Into Daily Life

Inner child healing is not a one-time process. It's a lifelong conversation. As you grow in awareness, you begin to build a relationship with this part of you — one rooted in love and trust.

With every mindful breath, every gentle response, every moment you choose presence over perfection — you are reparenting the child within.

This is what it means to reclaim your wholeness.

CHAPTER SIX

MINDFULNESS & STRESS MANAGEMENT

Transforming Pressure Into Presence

Stress is often described as the enemy of peace — but mindfulness reveals a deeper truth: stress isn't something to eliminate; it's something to understand. When approached mindfully, stress becomes a powerful teacher, illuminating our wounds, our limits, and our deepest unmet needs.

This chapter explores how to meet stress not with resistance, but with presence. With breath. With compassion.

What Is Stress, Really?

Stress is the body's natural response to perceived threat. It activates our nervous system — racing heart, shallow breath, muscle tension — in preparation to fight, flee, or freeze. This response is useful in emergencies, but in our modern world, the stress switch gets stuck on.

Deadlines, emails, unresolved trauma, constant comparison, overcommitment — they all whisper to the body: "You are not safe."

Mindfulness teaches the body and mind to return to safety. To breathe. To soften. To choose response over reaction.

Symptoms of Chronic Stress

- Restlessness or insomnia
- Physical pain or fatigue
- Emotional numbness or irritability
- Difficulty concentrating
- Feeling overwhelmed or "wired but tired"

These aren't signs of weakness. They're signs that your system is overloaded — and it's time to listen.

How Mindfulness Helps Regulate Stress

1. Nervous System Regulation

- Mindful breathing slows the heart rate and engages the parasympathetic (rest-and-digest) system.
- Regular meditation decreases cortisol and lowers blood pressure.

1. Emotional Awareness

- Mindfulness helps us track the onset of stress instead of being hijacked by it.
- By noticing stress early, we create space to respond gently.

3. Cognitive Reframing

- Instead of reacting with fear or frustration, we begin to see stress as a signal — "Something here needs care or change."

Practices for Stress Relief
1. Mindful Breathing Under Pressure
When you feel the surge of stress:

- Inhale deeply through the nose (4 seconds)
- Hold (2 seconds)
- Exhale slowly through the mouth (6 seconds)
Repeat 3–5 times. Feel your shoulders drop. Your jaw soften.

2. "Name it to Tame it"
Label your current emotional state:
"I'm feeling tense."
"I notice frustration."
This practice activates the logical part of the brain and decreases emotional overwhelm.
3. The 5-4-3-2-1 Grounding Practice
Use your senses to anchor in the now:

- 5 things you see
- 4 things you can touch
- 3 things you hear
- 2 things you smell

- 1 thing you taste

This pulls your awareness out of spiraling thoughts and into the safety of the present.

4. The "Sacred Pause"

Before reacting — pause.

Just one conscious breath can shift your entire nervous system. The pause gives you power. In that space, you reclaim yourself.

The Deeper Root: Is Your Inner Child Stressed?

Many adult stress patterns are rooted in childhood conditioning:

- Feeling you must always be perfect
- Needing to fix others to feel valuable
- Fearing disapproval or abandonment

Mindfulness lets us identify whose voice is reacting — and gently tend to that part of us. Often, the stressor is less about the situation and more about the wound it triggers.

Building a Stress-Resilient Lifestyle

- Create buffer space: Don't overschedule. Rest is productive.
- Return to nature: Even 10 minutes outside helps regulate cortisol.
- Eat and hydrate mindfully: Skipping meals = stress for the body.
- Digital boundaries: Protect your attention like it's sacred — because it is.

Mindfulness is not a quick fix. It's a lifestyle. A way of honoring your limits instead of pushing past them.

CHAPTER SEVEN

PRESENCE IN RELATIONSHIPS

Listening, Loving, and Setting Soulful Boundaries

Mindfulness isn't just about our inner world. It's also about how we show up in the shared spaces between us — in love, in friendship, in conflict, and in silence. Our presence becomes the foundation for conscious, compassionate relationships.

This chapter explores how mindfulness transforms the way we relate — with others and with ourselves — through attuned communication, deep listening, and healthy boundaries.

Connection Begins Within

We often seek from others what we've yet to offer ourselves — love, validation, acceptance, safety. The truth is, the relationship we have with ourselves sets the tone for every other connection in our lives.

When we're disconnected from our inner world, we:

- React instead of respond
- Project old wounds onto new people
- Struggle with boundaries or emotional expression

Mindfulness helps us come home to ourselves, so we can relate to others from wholeness instead of wounding.

Mindful Listening: Hearing Without Defending

One of the greatest gifts we can give someone is our full attention. Mindful listening means:

- Not interrupting
- Not preparing your rebuttal while they speak
- Being present with their energy, not just their words

Try this practice:

Breathe as they speak. Feel the breath anchor you in non-reactivity. When it's your turn, speak slowly and truthfully.

Communicating With Compassion

Mindful communication is both honest and kind. It involves:

- Speaking from "I" (e.g., "I feel..." instead of "You always...")
- Taking responsibility for your own triggers
- Pausing before speaking when emotions run high

Before responding, ask:

"Is what I'm about to say true, necessary, and kind?"

If not, wait. Silence can be more healing than words said in reaction.

Boundaries as Sacred Containers

Boundaries are not walls — they are bridges built with clarity and love. They protect your energy and support emotional safety.

Signs you need boundaries:

- You feel drained after being with certain people
- You say yes when you mean no
- You feel guilty for resting or needing space

Mindfulness helps you feel when your boundaries are being crossed — and gives you the courage to act with grace.

Practice: The Boundary Check-In

- "What's mine to carry?"
- "What am I doing out of obligation, not alignment?"
- "Where do I need to say no in order to say yes to myself?"

Conflict Through the Lens of Awareness

Conflict is inevitable, but suffering is optional. With mindfulness:

- We recognize when we're triggered and pause
- We breathe instead of blame
- We stay grounded in empathy, even when emotions run high

Sometimes, mindfulness means stepping away temporarily to return with clarity. That too is an act of love.

The Role of the Inner Child in Relationships

Old wounds show up in current connections. When we feel ignored, dismissed, or abandoned, it's often our inner child reacting.

Mindfulness helps you:

- Soften when old pain surfaces
- Communicate your needs with vulnerability
- Soothe your inner child before expecting someone else to

Try this when triggered:

Pause. Hand on heart. Ask, "How old do I feel right now?"

Then respond with the tenderness you needed back then.

Rituals for Deeper Connection

- Sacred Conversations: Weekly check-ins with loved ones without distractions
- Mindful Touch: Hug longer. Hold hands with presence.
- Gratitude Sharing: Name one thing you appreciate about the other daily
- Silent Togetherness: Be in the same room without talking, just being

When presence enters relationships, so does healing. Love deepens. Communication softens. And connection becomes less about control, and more about communion.

Enter Caption

CHAPTER EIGHT

MINDFULNESS AT WORK & IN THE MODERN WORLD

Staying Grounded in a World That Never Stops Moving

Our world is fast. Notifications ping, deadlines loom, and our worth is often measured in output. Amid all this, mindfulness becomes more than a practice — it becomes a lifeline.

In this chapter, we explore how to bring presence into environments that typically pull us out of ourselves: the workplace, the digital realm, and daily modern life.

Why We Need Mindfulness in the Modern World

We are more connected than ever — and yet, more distracted, anxious, and overwhelmed. The average attention span is shrinking, burnout is rising, and stillness is rare.

Mindfulness doesn't require us to abandon our lives. It invites us to return to them — awake, aware, and aligned.

When we infuse presence into daily routines, we begin to reclaim:

- Mental clarity
- Emotional regulation
- A sense of purpose beyond productivity

Mindfulness at Work

1. Start With Intention

Before checking emails or joining meetings, pause. Breathe. Ask:

- "What energy do I want to bring today?"
- "How can I respond rather than react?"

This simple shift can change the tone of your entire day.

2. Create Mindful Micro-Breaks

- Step away from your screen every 60–90 minutes
- Take 5 deep breaths while washing your hands
- Stand and stretch mindfully, tuning in to your body

These tiny rituals protect your nervous system from overstimulation.

3. Focus on One Thing at a Time

Multitasking fractures attention and increases stress. Try:

- Closing extra tabs
- Turning off non-urgent notifications
- Giving full presence to each task before moving on

Presence increases both peace and productivity.

Digital Mindfulness

We live in an age of constant consumption — information, content, opinions, urgency. Our devices often become extensions of our anxiety.

Practices to Stay Grounded:

- Digital sunrise: No phone for the first 30–60 minutes of your day
- Conscious consumption: Ask, "Is this nourishing me or numbing me?"
- Social media detox days: Step away to reconnect with what's real

Try setting your lock screen wallpaper to a mindful reminder: "Come back. You are here."

Redesigning Your Life With Presence

Mindfulness isn't about fitting in one more task — it's about transforming the way you live. Consider this:

- Schedule spaciousness: Don't pack your day wall-to-wall
- Batch and breathe: Group similar tasks, and take a pause in between
- Commute consciously: Turn off the radio, breathe deeply, observe the world around you

The goal is not to escape the modern world, but to meet it with grace.

When Work and Worth Are Entangled

Many of us carry old beliefs that our value comes from doing, achieving, performing. These wounds often begin in childhood and manifest in burnout and perfectionism.

Ask yourself:

- "Who am I without what I do?"
- "What am I seeking through overworking?"
- "What would it feel like to just be... enough?"

Mindfulness invites you to be, not just to do.

Creating a Grounding Workspace

- Keep a calming object nearby (crystal, leaf, photo, etc.)
- Use gentle lighting and reduce noise clutter when possible
- Take 3 breaths before starting each task
- Add a plant or natural element — nature soothes the nervous system

Your space becomes a reflection of your inner state — and vice versa.

The modern world isn't going to slow down. But you can.

And when you do, you shift your relationship with time, work, and life itself.

CHAPTER NINE

THE OBSTACLES TO PRESENCE

Navigating Resistance, Distraction, and Emotional Avoidance

Presence sounds simple — and in essence, it is. But the path to mindfulness isn't always smooth. In fact, the deeper we walk into awareness, the more we begin to meet the very patterns that have kept us disconnected.

This chapter gently explores those internal and external blocks — not as failures, but as doorways. Every obstacle to presence holds wisdom. Every resistance is a part of you asking to be seen.

Common Obstacles to Mindful Living

1. The "Monkey Mind"

This is the ever-chattering mind — jumping from thought to thought, memory to worry, to-do list to fantasy. It's not a problem to be fixed, but a pattern to understand.

Mindful Response: Instead of trying to silence it, observe it.

Label thoughts as "thinking" and return to the breath. Each time you notice, you've already succeeded.

2. Emotional Avoidance

Many people use busyness or distraction to avoid feeling — especially grief, anger, shame, or fear.

But mindfulness doesn't mean avoiding emotion. It means turning toward it, gently and with compassion.

Try This: When emotion arises, ask:

- "Where do I feel this in my body?"
- "What might this emotion need from me?"

Feelings soften when they are allowed.

3. The Perfectionist Within

The perfectionist says: "You must meditate perfectly. You must be calm all the time. If you mess up, you've failed."

This voice often stems from early experiences of conditional love or high expectations. It drives us to achieve rather than receive the moment.

Mindful Reframe: You are not practicing to be perfect. You are practicing to be present — with all your humanness.

4. Resistance to Stillness

Stillness can be uncomfortable, especially if you've lived in constant motion. For many, slowing down means meeting what's been buried.

If you find yourself fidgeting, distracting, or avoiding quiet time — that's resistance.

Respond with Kindness: Try shorter sessions. Pair stillness with gentle movement (like

walking meditation or slow yoga). Stillness is a muscle — build it with care.

5. Distraction Culture

Notifications. Content overload. Constant comparison. The modern world is designed to hijack attention.

Counter it with Conscious Design:

- Turn off non-essential alerts
- Schedule "scroll-free" hours
- Replace noise with silence at least once a day
- Protect your morning and evening routines like sacred rituals

Mindfulness in the digital age is an act of rebellion — and a return to self.

When Inner Wounds Disrupt Outer Peace

Sometimes the greatest blocks aren't outer distractions, but inner stories:

- "I don't deserve peace."
- "If I slow down, everything will fall apart."
- "Feeling is too painful — I'd rather stay numb."

These are not truths. They are traumas — echoes of unmet needs. Mindfulness helps us see them not as enemies, but as children at the door, asking to be loved.

Practice: Meeting Resistance with Presence

When you feel resistance to your practice, try this:

1. Name It: "I notice resistance. I don't want to sit today."
2. Ask It: "What are you afraid I'll feel if I slow down?"
3. Thank It: "Thank you for trying to protect me."
4. Invite It In: "You can stay, but I will sit anyway — even if just for one breath."

This approach creates trust with your inner system.

Presence isn't about eliminating resistance — it's about including it. Each time you meet a block with compassion, you reclaim a piece of yourself.

CHAPTER TEN

BUILDING A MINDFULNESS TOOLKIT

Creating Sacred Support for a Lifetime of Presence

Mindfulness is not a one-time transformation. It's a lifelong unfolding — a practice that grows with you, adapts to you, and becomes your steady companion through every season of life.

To support this journey, we need tools — not just techniques, but soul-anchored structures and sacred spaces that help us stay grounded when life inevitably becomes chaotic.

This chapter offers a gentle guide to building your own Mindfulness Toolkit — a personalized, flexible system that nourishes your body, calms your mind, and protects your energy.

1. Create a Sacred Space

You don't need a meditation hall or a mountain retreat. Just a small corner of your home, infused with intention, can become a sanctuary.

Include items that inspire calm and connection:

- A cushion or chair dedicated to stillness
- A candle, incense, or essential oil diffuser
- Nature objects — stones, leaves, shells, plants
- A journal and pen
- Photos, artwork, or symbols that hold meaning

The key is consistency — let this space become a portal that signals: Here, I return to myself.

2. Mindfulness Apps & Digital Tools

Used with intention, technology can support presence instead of hijacking it.

Recommended Apps:

- Insight Timer: Free meditations and calming music

- Headspace: Guided mindfulness series for beginners
- Calm: Breathwork, sleep aids, and stress relief
- Aura or Simple Habit: Short mindfulness breaks throughout the day

Set gentle reminders during your day to pause and return to your breath.

3. Mindfulness Objects

Tactile tools can help ground you when your mind is scattered.
Try:

- A smooth grounding stone you hold during anxiety
- Mala or prayer beads for breath-counting
- A small bell to mark the start/end of practice
- A "pause card" in your wallet with a simple reminder: "Breathe. Return."

Even a warm cup of tea held mindfully can become a sacred object.

4. Rituals That Anchor Your Day

Presence is not something we stumble into — it's something we create space for.

Morning Rituals:

- Sit in silence before touching your phone
- Journal 3 mindful intentions for the day
- Breathe deeply for 2 minutes while watching the light shift

Evening Rituals:

- Reflect on one moment of gratitude from the day
- Do a short body scan to release tension
- Whisper a kind word to your inner child before sleep

Weekly Rituals:

- Mindful walks in nature
- A personal "Sabbath" with no digital input
- Time to reset your space and energy

5. Build Your Support System

Mindfulness is powerful alone — but it deepens in community.

Options to Explore:

- Attend local meditation circles or online sanghas (spiritual communities)
- Join mindfulness challenges or retreats
- Share your journey with a trusted friend or therapist
- Start a small group where you check in weekly with presence-based questions

Support doesn't mean dependence — it means mirroring and encouragement. Your journey becomes less lonely and more alive.

6. Self-Compassion Practices for Lifelong Healing

Every practice in your toolkit must include grace. You will forget. You will resist. That's okay.

In those moments, return to:

- Your breath
- A grounding affirmation
- A loving voice inside that says: "Begin again."

This is the true heart of the practice.
Try This: The "Mindfulness Toolkit Inventory"
Write out your toolkit:

- My grounding space: ________
- My go-to practices: ________
- My emotional anchors: ________
- My reminders or symbols: ________
- My community or support: ________

Update it monthly. Let it evolve with you.

This toolkit isn't about adding more tasks. It's about creating a sacred rhythm — one that helps you live intentionally, love deeply, and walk through the world with peace in your breath and presence in your soul.

CHAPTER ELEVEN

THE 21-DAY MINDFULNESS RECLAIMED CHALLENGE

Daily Healing. Gentle Awareness. Coming Home to the Present.

?

Welcome to the Challenge

You've journeyed through deep awareness, inner healing, and compassionate presence. Now, it's time to live it — not all at once, but breath by breath, one mindful day at a time.

? Mindfulness Reclaimed: 21-Day Challenge

Week 1: Coming Back to the Present

Day 1 – Grounding with Breath

Practice: 5-minute focused breathing.

Prompt: *What did I notice when I focused on my breath?*

Day 2 – Body Scan Awareness

Practice: 10-minute body scan (lying or sitting).

Prompt: *What part of my body felt most tense or relaxed?*

Day 3 – Digital Detox Moment

Practice: Stay offline for 2 hours today.

Prompt: *How did I feel being unplugged?*

Day 4 – Eat with Intention

Practice: Eat one meal mindfully—no distractions.

Prompt: *What flavors or sensations did I notice more clearly?*

Day 5 – Listening Deeply

Practice: Have one conversation where you fully listen without interrupting.

Prompt: *How did this change the connection?*

Day 6 – Observe Nature

Practice: Spend 10 minutes in nature just observing.

Prompt: *What surprised me about the natural world today?*

Day 7 – Mindful Music or Silence

Practice: Listen to calming music or sit in silence.

Prompt: *What emotions or thoughts arose during this time?*

Week 2: Reclaiming Inner Space

Day 8 – Journal Your Mind

Practice: Free-write for 10 minutes.

Prompt: *What themes keep surfacing in my thoughts?*

Day 9 – Mindful Walking

Practice: Walk slowly, paying attention to your steps and surroundings.

Prompt: *How did walking mindfully shift my energy?*

Day 10 – Letting Go Practice

Practice: Write down one worry and tear it up.

Prompt: *How did it feel to symbolically release it?*

Day 11 – Touchstone Object

Practice: Hold or wear something meaningful and focus on it during stress.

Prompt: *What strength or memory does this item evoke?*

Day 12 – Create Something

Practice: Draw, write, cook—anything creative.

Prompt: *What came through when I allowed creativity in?*

Day 13 – Affirmation Anchor

Practice: Choose one calming affirmation to repeat throughout the day.

Prompt: *How did this shape my mindset?*

Day 14 – Be with Stillness

Practice: Sit for 10 minutes doing absolutely nothing.

Prompt: *What did stillness reveal to me today?*

Week 3: Integrating Mindfulness into Life

Day 15 – Morning Mindset Check-In

Practice: Start your day by setting an intention.

Prompt: *What do I want to embody today?*

Day 16 – Mindfulness in Chores

Practice: Wash dishes, sweep, fold laundry mindfully.

Prompt: *How did mindfulness shift this routine task?*

Day 17 – Gratitude Walk

Practice: Walk and silently name things you're grateful for.

Prompt: *What felt most heart-opening on this walk?*

Day 18 – Self-Compassion Pause

Practice: When you make a mistake, pause and offer yourself kindness.

Prompt: *What would I say to a friend in the same situation?*

Day 19 – Mindful Media Moment

Practice: Choose one piece of content (book, video, podcast) that nourishes

Prompt: *How did this inspire or ground me?*

Day 20 – Connect Consciously

Practice: Reach out to someone with full attention—no multitasking.

Prompt: *How did presence affect the connection?*

Day 21 – Celebrate the Journey

Practice: Reflect on your growth over the past 21 days.

Prompt: *What have I reclaimed? What will I carry forward?*

CHAPTER TWELVE

Reflections and Closing Thoughts
A Final Breath Before You Continue Alone

A Note from the Path

"You don't have to hustle your way into peace. You just have to stop long enough to remember — it's already within you." If this journey has shown you anything, let it be this: You are not alone in your overwhelm. You are not broken because you struggle. And you are not behind if your healing is slow. Whether you're a corporate leader navigating burnout, a parent raising children in a hyper-digital world, or a survivor learning how to feel safe in your own body again — mindfulness meets you where you are. Not to fix you. But to walk with you. To remind you that:

• You can pause.
• You can soften.
• You can begin again.

May mindfulness become your ally, not just in calm moments — but especially in messy ones. This practice is not about becoming a better version of yourself. It's about remembering the version of you that was always whole. You're doing better than you think. You're more resilient than you know. And your breath is always waiting for you to return.

With stillness & strength

Sthitipragyan Mohanty

About The Author

Enter Caption

Sthitipragyan Mohanty is a corporate professional turned social activist, mindfulness trainer, and conscious living advocate. With over a decade of experience in the corporate world, Sthitipragyan Mohanty made a powerful shift toward a more intentional life—one rooted in presence, purpose, and peace.

A certified trainer in POSH (Prevention of Sexual Harassment), POCSO (Protection of Children from Sexual Offences), and meditation, Sthitipragyan Mohanty brings a holistic and heart-centered approach to personal transformation. Their work centres around helping people reclaim their inner calm, rewire their thoughts, and return to what truly matters.

As the founder of OdraTales, an e-commerce platform dedicated to promoting sustainable clothing and reviving traditional crafts, Sthitipragyan Mohanty is also deeply committed to cultural preservation and conscious fashion. OdraTales empowers artisans and weavers across Odisha by giving them a platform to share their stories, skills, and heritage with the world.

This book, *Mindfulness Reclaimed*, is a reflection of Sthitipragyan Mohanty's own journey—a guide to finding stillness in the noise, reclaiming attention in an age of distraction, and living more mindfully in every sense of the word.

When not writing or leading mindfulness sessions, she can be found walking barefoot in nature, listening to silence, or exploring handwoven fabrics that tell ancestral tales.

https://mindfulnesslivingblog.wordpress.com/

www.ingramcontent.com/pod-product-compliance
Lightning Source LLC
Chambersburg PA
CBHW031245130726
47988CB00008B/3242